MW00476169

In this delightful little book, Jonathan Pennington proves himself at home in the library and the pulpit. He draws on an array of disciplines to produce clear, helpful counsel on preparation, writing, fears ("This Sermon Stinks"), praise, and criticism. And don't miss his consummate instruction on the first and last minutes of a sermon.

—**Dan Doriani**, Professor of Theology and Vice President, Covenant Theological Seminary

Jonathan Pennington's *Small Preaching* is an enormous help to preachers who want to sharpen their skills, deepen their thinking, and amplify their effectiveness. This book beautifully combines the renowned exegetical and hermeneutical skills of an eminent New Testament scholar with the heart and passion of a shepherd who loves God's flock."

—**Hershael W. York**, Dean of the School of Theology and Victor and Louise Lester Professor of Preaching, The Southern Baptist Theological Seminary, and Senior Pastor, Buck Run Baptist Church

Compact wisdom. Winsome word pictures. Benefits for beginners, veterans, and those in between. These bite-sized essays are easy to sink your teeth into. Take them in, whether as 25 snacks or a balanced meal. Your listeners will bless you.

—**Greg Scharf**, Professor Emeritus of Homiletics and Pastoral Theology, Trinity Evangelical Divinity school, author of *Prepared to Preach* and *Let the Earth Hear His Voice*

Small things done consistently over time can have a massive impact. In *Small Preaching*, Jonathan Pennington advocates that minor changes can have a big impact on preachers and their preaching. This book will help preachers who are just starting to hone their skills and seasoned ministers alike.

—**J T English**, Lead Pastor, Storyline Fellowship

This book is unlike any other book on preaching I've ever read. For years, Pennington has taught us how to read the Gospels wisely. In this book, he teaches us how to preach the gospel wisely. Intensely practical and specific, this book is a treasure trove of hard-won insights from a seasoned preacher still in the trenches. Focusing on the preacher as much as the preaching, Pennington skillfully fills in some of the most crucial gaps that often get left out of conversations and instruction about preaching. I plan to make it mandatory reading for all the pastors and leaders I have the opportunity to serve and teach.

—**Beau Hughes**, Lead Pastor, The Village Church Denton

Small Preaching is a purposefully modest, even humble, approach to a task that requires a great deal of humility. Pennington so helpfully reminds us that preaching is a "slow art" and he pays attention to things not usually covered in traditional books on preaching, things which, nonetheless, are so much a part of the real life of the preaching task. This book is stimulating and provocative, and it will make you think about your preaching. That, in turn, will bear good fruit, maybe even as soon as this coming Sunday.

—**Mike Bullmore**, Senior Pastor, Crossway Community Church

Pastors do not need another preaching book that simply affirms the significance and impact of preaching. The book you hold in your hands is different. Jonathan Pennington has written a very helpful, practical, accessible, and uniquely insightful little book that I am convinced has something for every pastor to help him grow in his preaching ministry. And do not be surprised if you find yourself personally challenged in ways that many preaching books fall short and several pastors fail to examine in their own souls. *Small Preaching* may be small in size and length, but not in the practical wisdom of which all pastors desire and need. I commend it to every pastor."

—**Brian Croft**, Founder and Executive Director Practical Shepherding

Small
Preaching

Small
Preaching

25 Little Things
You Can Do Now
to Become
a Better Preacher

◆

JONATHAN T.
PENNINGTON

LEXHAM PRESS

Small Preaching: 25 Little Things You Can Do Now to Become a Better Preacher

Copyright 2021 Jonathan T. Pennington

Lexham Press, 1313 Commercial St., Bellingham, WA 98225
LexhamPress.com

Print ISBN 9781683594710
Digital ISBN 9781683594727
Library of Congress Control Number 2020950472

Lexham Editorial: Elliot Ritzema, Andrew Sheffield, Jessi Strong
Cover Design: Lydia Dahl
Typesetting: Justin Marr

To Tracy Pennington, who has faithfully listened to a lot of sermons from me over twenty-five years, and whose advice has been immeasurably valuable. The effectiveness of any of my sermons is directly tied to whether I listened to her brilliant pre-run advice on Saturday night or not!

Emphasis on balance in first section

Contents

The Practice of Preaching

Introduction

"Small" is not a particularly positive word in most instances. Who wants a small bank account, a small amount of honor, or a job with a small salary or a small number of benefits? And even though we might romanticize some advantages to having a small church, I think few pastors in their honest moments would rather have their church be small than large and growing.

When it comes to preaching, I'll go out on a (small) limb to suggest that no one has ever put "small" and "preaching" together in a positive sense. One unscientific bit of supportive data is that in an age when any potentially marketable website domain name has been snatched up by squatters hoping to make a quick buck, www.smallpreaching.com was readily available to me. (I now own it, so don't get any ideas. In fact, check it out for some great resources.)

But "small" can be good and even revolutionary. Think of "small ball" as practiced during the 2013–2014 season by the Kansas City Royals in baseball or the Golden State Warriors in basketball. The Royals used a "small ball" strategy to show that a team can be very successful without a beefy budget or highly paid home run sluggers. They employed a technique of small, methodical steps—base hits, bunts, stolen bases, sacrifice flies—to get runners on base and around to home. And it worked. Similarly, the Warriors, instead of concentrating on having the "big man" underneath the basket, found great success through fast-paced offense with multiple agile dribblers and shooters.

In his excellent book *Small Teaching*, James Lang applies the idea of "small" to help teachers become more effective at what they do.[1] Lang, a professor himself, knows that most teachers want to develop their skills and become more engaging and effective, but doing so is difficult. Conferences, books, and seminars promise that a radical overhaul of education and pedagogy will solve all of our problems as teachers. Lang, however, rightly argues that it is not possible for teachers and professors to change everything they do—to flip every classroom, to revamp an entire school, to jettison all they have been taught. Instead, it is far more wise, realistic, and effectual to make small steps—methodical little changes to how a teacher approaches teaching and learning. It's a "small ball" approach to improved pedagogy, and it works.

Small ball. Small teaching. And now, small preaching. Occupationally, I am both a professor and a preacher, and I care about both of these roles very much. I give a lot of my time and energy to focusing on what these two roles share—the importance of excellence and beauty in the act of communication. I'm also aware of the many challenges that preachers face as they live out their calling. If you're reading this book, you probably care about all of this too.

My goal in this book is to help you make some small ball/ small teaching steps toward intentionally better preaching. This is not a book about a whole philosophy and practice of preaching. There are plenty of good books out there like that, and I have been inspired and helped by many of them. If you ever took a homiletics course in seminary, you got your professor's own version of that, I'm sure. Instead, this is a book of small ideas that you can try today.

How does lasting change come about in diet or exercise or acquiring a new skill? Through taking small steps in the same direction over time. This book does not promise that if you just do this one thing, then your preaching will magically be different, the preaching version of hiring the $200 million slugger or the 7'2" center. Instead, I offer you here some small ideas that can have big consequences if you play the long and methodical game with sincerity and intentionality.

Small Preaching is a collection of twenty-five short, easily digestible essays that invite you to see and be in the world in certain ways. These nugget-sized explorations are organized under three headings, complete with pleasant "p's" and alluring alliteration: The Person of the Preacher, The Preparation for Preaching, and The Practice of Preaching. The essays you'll find here are varied in their approaches, topics, content, and modes. Some cast vision; some challenge assumptions and habits; some give "pro tips" gleaned from experts. But all invite you to consider small changes that can add up to big effect, no matter whether you are about to start at your first church, or are an old pro. So come and start small.

The Person
of the Preacher

◆ 1 ◆

Handling Praise Carefully and Gladly

We humans, made in the image of the relational Triune God, need the encouragement and love of others. There was only a brief and singular time when a human was completely alone in creation, and God's verdict was clear: "It's not good for the human to be alone" (Genesis 2:18).

Humans—including the small subspecies of humanity who are called to preach—need the encouragement and love of other humans. "The worker is worthy of his wages" (1 Timothy 5:18) applies not only financially but also relationally and emotionally. Praise is a good and natural need. ? It is a sustaining gift.

Most preachers I've observed are hesitant to receive praise and compliments. This is a mistake. But at the same time, the pastor needs to think carefully about how to handle praise in a healthy way.

We can sum up the healthy reception of preaching praise with two adverbs: *carefully and gladly*.

Carefully. There are a couple of reasons why we must be wisely careful about how we receive praise. First, what Emily Dickinson says about fame applies more generally to all forms of praise:

> Fame is a bee.
> It has a song—
> It has a sting—
> Ah, too, it has a wing.[2]

Fame and praise are fleeting and fickle. Beware of putting much stock in the praise of others. Hold it all at arm's length lest you be throat-punched when its inevitable cousin criticism shows up.

A second reason we must be careful in our reception of praise is that it is an addictive drug that can blind us to the ultimately important praise—the praise and honor that come from God himself. In Matthew 6:1–21, Jesus teaches at length on the danger of seeking the praise of others. Our problem is *not* the natural human desire for reward or praise. Our problem is our drive and love for getting praise from the wrong place. If we treasure up the earthly reward of people praising us, we will find ourselves with *only* that treasure, not a reward from God. Where our treasure is, there our heart is, too. So open carefully the gift of praise.

Gladly. Most preachers are aware of the dangers of praise, and most of us are not going to openly seek praise in a crass and obviously self-promoting way. (Though subtle compliment-seeking and praise-fishing are much more common. Guilty as charged.) This good piety and humility, however, can lead us to struggle to embrace the other, balancing aspect of praise reception: receiving it gladly.

It is good, natural, and beneficial to be the recipient of praise. This is a basic and non-sinful human need. Moreover, as Scripture teaches, we should give honor where honor is due. A preacher who is called and gifted and who labors at the craft of preaching is worthy of appropriate and healthy honor. Only an unbiblical altruism eschews this way that God has made the universe: good begets good; labor begets honor; those who sow diligence should harvest its fruit. So we should not be hesitant or resistant to receive compliments on our preaching. This is a gift not to be rejected. It is good and right.

So what do you say when someone compliments you in person or in an email? I embrace these moments with gratitude and say some combination of these things:

- "I'm glad to hear that you benefited from the message. Thank you!"

- "You're very kind. Thank you for taking the time to encourage me."

- "That's very nice to hear. I need encouragement like everyone else."

It is not humility to dismiss or deflect the compliment: "Oh, it's not me! Only God gets the credit!" This dishonors your gift and God's structure of the universe. When someone thanks you for your sermon, receive this good and beautiful gift, completing the cycle of giving and receiving that God has created.

The way of wisdom is always a knife's edge; it is easier to fall off one side or the other than to maintain the balanced walk. Our relationship to preaching praise should partake in neither the foolishness of self-aggrandizement nor the false humility of self-degradation. Praise is like food in that neither gluttony nor starvation is good. The wise preacher will look at praise not as an idolatrous source of life but as a gift that enables a healthy life. Don't be afraid of receiving praise, but handle it both carefully and gladly.

2

Handling Criticism
Carefully and Humbly

If you're going into the role of preaching expecting unending gift baskets and ticker-tape parades from grateful congregants telling you how much better you are than their last pastor—well, I'm not sure what to say except that maybe a career in metallurgy or something else far away from pastoring might be a better bet for you.

I imagine few preachers really expect perpetual praise. Nonetheless, when criticism comes—especially from unexpected people and at already-down times—it surprises and hurts us. And not only does it cause us personal pain, but also, I suggest that how you handle criticism will most often be the deciding factor in whether you survive at a church and in ministry overall. How you handle criticism is that important. Criticism that doesn't make you stronger will definitely kill you. To ensure that criticism makes you stronger, handle it *carefully and humbly*.

Carefully. Preaching is a performance, not in the negative sense but in the broader meaning of discharging or executing a public task or skill. It is inherent to preaching that you are putting your very self in front of people for scrutiny. So it is unavoidable that your ideas, your positions, your abilities, your mannerisms, your clothing, and your skills will be evaluated. And sooner or later (usually sooner), someone is going to say something critical, large or small, fair or unfair, based on insight or ignorance.

Whatever the form, time, type, or source, you should handle criticism *carefully*. This means, first of all, <u>decide that you will not respond immediately</u>. Maybe you see the cranky old guy coming toward you across the sanctuary for his weekly criticism appointment. Or maybe it is a tiny comment heard thirdhand from someone you thought liked you. Either way, in that moment, take a deep breath and imagine yourself in a posture that is open armed, not fists raised. Don't fight back. Don't defend yourself. Develop the self-control to not get triggered in the moment. If all you can say back is "Okay," then that's enough for now. If it is appropriate and you can in the moment, it may be even better to respond with "Thank you. I'll think about that." A gentle answer turns away most wrath, but a harsh response stirs up more criticism.

Then, when you have a chance to think, carefully and prayerfully consider the criticism in all its aspects—source, form, and content. Imagine the criticism as a virtual object (not a person) outside of yourself that you can examine, turning it over and looking at it from all sides. Some criticisms can and should be immediately thrown out the window. (And don't go out to retrieve them.) Some criticisms are on point and should be examined more. Some need to be stripped down to a nugget of truth to heed. But you must carefully consider the criticism with the studied eye of wisdom. Blindly ignoring criticism and letting it guide your every move are equally foolish and dangerous.

Humbly. God opposes the proud but gives grace to the humble (Psalm 138:6; James 4:6; 1 Peter 5:5). This creation-deep truism is repeated throughout Holy Scripture for a reason: lack of humility is destructive. Arrogance (and its wimpy brother, defensiveness) is the opposite of who God is and how his world works.

There is no place where humility is needed more or where its purity is tested further than in the smelting fire of criticism. So when you face criticism, welcome it with humility as a guest and a gift.

The first step in humbly receiving criticism is to see it as an opportunity for growth. I know this is hard, and that's why I said you must objectify the criticism. This will give you the psychological space to learn from it what you can. Ask, "What is true about the content of the criticism? What can I do better?" Alternatively, "What can I not change about myself and learn to live with?"

Pressing further, use it as a window into your own soul's health: "Why does this particular criticism upset me? What fears, insecurities, or shame does this evoke in me?" Once you can start to do this level of humble and honest soul work, real growth can take place. Humility tills the soil of your soul, and criticism can be the manure that fertilizes robust growth.

If after this self-examination there is an aspect of the criticism worth pursuing, in humility go to a few trusted friends and ask them what they think. Is this criticism something to consider more, to learn from, to prompt a change? God will give great grace to this kind of humility in community

The life of the preacher contains moments of great joy and satisfaction and moments of self-doubt and pain. Criticism from others can be devastating and haunting. I've noticed how even a small critique can lodge in my soul like a popcorn husk in my gums, providing constant irritation and provoking obsessive work to remove it. Failure to handle criticism well will destroy us and, thereby, our ministries. But it doesn't have to be so. Even as we can grow in homiletical skill, we can grow in learning to handle criticism carefully and humbly.

3

Band of Brothers Preaching

On October 25, 1415, Saint Crispin's Day, English King Henry V stood before his army of roughly 9,000 near the village of Agincourt, intercepted by a French force of 36,000. Shakespeare retells Henry's famous speech to his men inspiring them to rejoice and bravely go into the day's battle because they would always be remembered, either by their scars or in their deaths. Henry proclaims that all who did not fight at the battle on Saint Crispin's Day would be jealous of "we few; we happy few; we band of brothers."

This speech has continued to inspire, including when it was broadcast across radio sets in England during the dark days of World War II. The speech has also lent its phrase "band of brothers" to many a story, including the account of a company of paratroopers, led by Major Richard Winters, who landed at Normandy and fought all the way to Hitler's headquarters, the *Kehlsteinhaus*. The deeply felt camaraderie that comes from living together through trials is one of humanity's core transformative experiences.

At the risk of sounding overly dramatic or triumphalistic, ⌐I want to inspire us pastors to think about ourselves as a preaching band of brothers.⌐To preach as a band of brothers means you <u>reorient your preaching life around</u> an <u>intentional interdependence</u>. I am inviting you to recognize that to scale the monumental task of the preaching life, we need a close-knit group of like-missioned people working together. ⌐We need more than our respectful congregants and staff.⌐We need a group of other preachers in our lives who are of one company. We need this few, this happy few, this band of brothers, and we need it not just at annual conferences but on a weekly basis.

What I mean is that preachers should develop habits of working together on sermon preparation through sharing illustrations, outlines, and applications. I mean that preachers should cultivate patterns of regular dialogue with other preachers. Band-of-brothers preachers can share resources and plan to preach parallel series at their own churches, thus gaining from the synergy of wrestling with texts together. This means neither independence nor overdependence but a truly banded, interdependent approach to the life of preaching.

Why should we do this? I hope it is immediately apparent that such an approach—as uncommon as it has been in recent decades—is a great source of encouragement, stimulation, accountability, and growth. The sum preaching of the preachers will be stronger than the individual parts.

The bond of the band of brothers is stronger than even the strongest preacher's gifts and abilities. Certainly, some in such a group may feel intimidated because some will be more talented and have more to offer than others, but this is okay. This is how life always is. If our vision is truly for the advancement of God's kingdom and not our own self-aggrandizement, such a uniting together to strengthen all is good and beautiful.

For some time, I experienced an ideal version of this with the network of churches in my city. Built into this system was a commitment to preach through the same series and texts each week. We shared commentaries and other resources, and we gathered weekly to discuss our ideas and plans. Each sermon was the work of each preacher—don't plagiarize, please!—but each sermon benefitted from the group's collective wisdom, interpretive wrestling, and homiletical moves. I often had a breakthrough at these meetings or got a choice line or quote from my brothers laboring with the same text toward the same looming Sunday morning.

For most preachers, this ideal situation is not a possibility. That's okay. There is still great potential for gathering together a small band of preachers. First, this can be done in a broader area. Find a group within fifty miles, cast the vision for this, take the lead in organizing it, and make it happen. Many pastors would be very willing to give half a day to gather together with other like-minded people and get help thinking through and improving their sermons. This would require some planning ahead of sermon series, but the effort will more than pay off. If meeting in person does not seem possible, make it happen digitally. Gather together some brothers from far and wide and commit to a weekly video call. With today's technology, this is very doable.

Pray about it. Try it. Begin dreaming about what this could be and step toward it. No soldier wins a battle by himself. Be the King Henry or the Major Winters who leads a band of brothers toward the humble advancing of God's kingdom in the world.

Metaphor of battle

♦ 4 ♦

Pastoring as Conducting

For those not trained in the world of classical music, it can be hard to understand and appreciate the role of an orchestra conductor. Of the hundred-or-so performers in a modern symphony, the maestro is the most honored—he or she is pictured on all the posters and receives the grand applauding entrance and ovations. Yet the conductor seems to do the least work of all! Conductors play no instrument and sing no notes but instead wave their hands wildly around, telling everyone else what to do.

What does a conductor really do? Going as far back as ancient Greece, we know of one Pherekydes of Patrae who used a golden staff to lead a group of some eight hundred musicians, keeping them together in time as they performed. Today, a large modern orchestra could not function—or at least not very well—without a maestro, and the best orchestras are recognized as the best largely because of their conductors. This is because the conductor leads, guides, unifies, and shapes the whole orchestra, without playing a single note during the concert.

A group of scientists studied the relationship between the conductor and musicians, analyzing the pattern of a conductor's signals by attaching infrared sensors to both the conductor's baton and the violinists' bows. They found that different conductors shaped "sensorimotor conversations" between the orchestra and themselves that were visually different, and these differences correlated to the power of the music. The more experienced conductors created music that was noticeably more aesthetically pleasing.[3] Maestros matter.

So what does this have to do with pastoring and preaching? Very much. The pastor's role can be helpfully compared to that of the conductor, with preaching as analogous to the performance. The good conductor prepares, listens, and leads. So too the pastor.

Prepare. Even though an hours-long orchestra performance may require sweat and energy from conductors, this is only the smallest part of what conductors actually do. Most of the conductor's time is given to preparation for the concert. Conductors have spent years mastering at least one instrument themselves and becoming deeply acquainted with them all—strings, brass, woodwinds, percussion, vocals. The conductor is the master interpreter of a complex musical text, and this interpretation requires research that is often rigorously academic. This includes studying the time period of the music, the biography of the composer, and how others have interpreted and performed the piece. As one expert has observed, "Like all the great mysteries, the mystery that is music only comes from huge amounts of hard work."[4]

So too the pastor. The Sunday morning sermon—the word proclaimed—is simultaneously an incredibly important single moment of the church's life and the smallest part of it. The pastor's preparation is what makes the preaching moment what it is. This preparation includes a lifetime of study of both Holy Scripture and human experience. Both academic labor (past education and weekly study) and pastoral care (living with and loving real people) are the necessary preparation for conducting the weekly service.

Listen. Maybe it is surprising to learn that a big part of what makes a great conductor is practiced and attentive listening. Have you ever seen what a conductor's score looks like? The other musicians are following along with their own printed notes; the conductor is looking at *everyone's* parts simultaneously on a massive musical score. And he is listening to all of them, detecting and directing them to work together. As author Tom Service notes, the conductor becomes the focal point, the "lightning rod of listening," so that "the players and the conductor can become something bigger than all of them—than all of us—at the same time as feeling fully realized as individuals."[5]

So too the pastor. The message delivered and the advice given are important, but they will only be authentic and effective if they are first rooted in attentive listening to the music that each person can and does contribute to the whole. When pastors try to lead and preach without first and continually listening, they become disconnected and often take the dangerous road of heavy-handed authoritarianism to preserve their position. Instead, powerful pastoring and preaching starts with aware listening, becoming the conduit used by God to listen to and speak with God's people.

Lead. Only after preparation and listening can a conductor lead. This leading is essential to the function of the whole orchestra because the maestro keeps everyone in time together through a unifying vision, an interpretation of the piece of music that is coherent and directed. Playing music is more than hitting the right notes. Musical performance involves interpretation and expression that vary by player and instrument. The conductor provides the necessary shared vision that brings together a diverse group of experts and individuals so that they can create complex music through the harmony of diversity while maintaining a coherent voice.

So too the pastor. The church is full of a wide variety of people, and this should be celebrated. It is precisely the diversity and differences among individuals that enable health, vitality, and beauty. The good pastor and preacher will lead these individuals toward not monophonic blandness but a shared contribution to the world that is shaped by the pastor's (God-given) vision. Leading like a conductor looks like directing diversity into harmony.

The apostle Paul writes that God has given teachers to the church "to equip God's people for works of service, so that the body of Christ may be built up" (Ephesians 4:12). The pastor/conductor is the leader, providing instruction and shaping vision. But the goal, and the evidence, of good pastoring/conducting is not the preaching performance but the effect—powerful music that adds beauty to the world.

And this is also the source of life for the pastor/conductor. As Benjamin Zander observes, the power and life of conductors are not in the noise they make but in their crucial role in empowering and directing the noise, in enabling others to sing and play.[6]

Preaching is not the only way the pastor leads, but it is the most visible and consistent way. The good preacher will remember that every sermonic performance is more than the content of the biblical text. Every sermon is an opportunity for the pastor to conduct his congregation well through preparing, listening, and leading.

metaphor of symphony

◆ 5 ◆

Be God's Witness, Not His Lawyer

E. Stanley Jones (1884–1973) has rightly been called the Billy Graham of India. Jones served as a Methodist missionary and teacher in that country throughout the crucial first half of the twentieth century. He became close personal friends with Gandhi and labored to contextualize Christianity into Indian culture in a respectful way. His book *The Christ of the Indian Road* had a significant impact on missions, and Jones was honored—including a Nobel Prize nomination—for his efforts to bring peace and mutual understanding between India and the West.

One of Jones's most famous quotes sums up what he learned through years of dialogical listening and speaking with Indians: "As God's lawyer I was a dead failure; as God's witness I was a success. ... [The Christian minister] is to be, not God's lawyer, to argue well for God; but he is to be God's witness, to tell what Grace has done for an unworthy life."[7]

I want to offer three readings of these stimulating words: one bad reading, one implication that Jones intended, and one further application.

First, the bad reading: Jones is not saying, nor would I suggest, that preaching must always lack argumentation or reasoning. Or to say it more clearly: Christian preaching and teaching will inevitably involve logical arguments, reasoning, explanation, and explication of what Christianity is. The exposition of what Holy Scripture says and what the gospel teaches is central to Christian witness—and Jones certainly agreed! This is not what he meant by avoiding lawyering. So whatever else one thinks Jones is saying, this quote is not pitting reason or argument against witnessing.

Second, the implication: So, what is Jones saying? His contrast between being "God's lawyer" and "God's witness" is rich with implication, namely, that no one is persuaded to follow Jesus by argumentation alone. No one is argued into the kingdom of God. Rather, it is the *testimony* of God's active and transforming grace in one's life that is the ultimate and most important "argument" for the truth of Christianity. As Jones discovered when trying to re-contextualize the whole Bible into a very foreign Indian culture, there were many things that were difficult to explain and make sense of. But he came to see that was okay. Above and beyond his ability to be God's defense lawyer was Jones's witness to God's grace in his life. Reasoning and testimony are not mutually exclusive, but neither are they equal in power and importance. It's better to be a good witness than a winning lawyer.

Third, one further application: We are not God's prosecuting attorneys. When we stand as self-appointed lawyers in the name of God, seeking to prosecute his people and the world, we take on the role of the Holy Spirit (John 16:8), not the role of the preacher. The role of the preacher is to witness to God's word and work in the world. The Holy Spirit is the one who convicts and brings repentance.

Preaching will at times include a prophetic call, a rebuke, or a challenge (though probably less often than some of us think). But preachers cannot bring about true conviction or repentance; that is a work of the Spirit. And when we try to do the Spirit's work, it always backfires.

The crucial difference between being God's lawyer and being his witness lies in how the preacher perceives his relationship with his hearers. Donning the mantle of (prosecuting) lawyer establishes an adversarial posture, while the calling of being a witness is a place of love—standing alongside others, pointing the way ahead to God, inviting people to God.

Therein is freedom and power. Lawyers attack positions, treat people with suspicion, marshal arguments about what should be, and seek to win as the goal. Faithful witnesses take a different role, one of humble and centered testimony to the truth they have seen and known. Be God's witness; he doesn't need any lawyers. *metaphor of courtroom*

◆ 6 ◆

Distinguishing between Preaching and Teaching

I recently had lunch with a former student who is now ten years into planting a growing inner-city church. He was asking my advice about how to build an educational plan that would provide his people with a richer and broader theological education. He was lamenting that there was so much his people needed to learn. His sermons were already long and often complicated, and he felt the need to say even more. My advice to him: You're trying to do too much in your sermons. *Preach* shorter sermons and *teach* in other venues.

This good pastor's problem—one that is common for all of us who value theological education—is that he had not yet gotten clear in his mind the important distinction between *preaching* and *teaching*. As a result of this conflation, he was trying to do things with his sermons that can only be done with teaching, to the detriment of both his preaching and his church members' growth.

What is the distinction? We can define preaching as *the invitational and exhortational proclamation of biblical and theological truth*. Teaching, by contrast, is *the explanation and explication of biblical and theological truth*.

What is shared between Christian preaching and teaching is the content—biblical and theological truth. The difference lies in the mode and immediate goal. Preaching is biblical and theological content selected and presented in a mode of proclamation with the immediate goal of invitation and exhortation. Teaching is biblical and theological content presented in a more detailed and systematic way for the purpose of explaining and unpacking complex issues, their interconnectedness, and their implications. There is overlap, but there is also distinction.

But such verbal definitions only get us so far. It is also helpful to conceptualize the relationship of preaching and teaching with a Venn diagram.

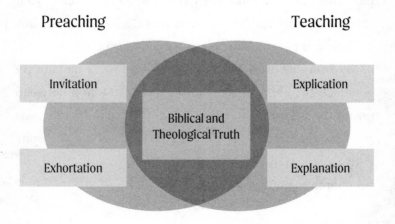

Preaching   Teaching

Invitation   Explication

Biblical and
Theological Truth

Exhortation   Explanation

Both preaching and teaching communicate biblical and theological truth, but their modes and goals are different.

We can also approach the preaching-teaching distinction from another angle: Preaching is monological, while teaching is dialogical. Preaching is communication that moves in only one direction, from the preacher in the pulpit to the hearers in the pews. (Even in a vibrantly interactive setting such as is common in the black church, the content is given by the preacher while the congregation provides vocal, and sometimes musical, encouragement.)

Teaching, on the other hand, if done well, is dialogical by nature. The communication of content is driven by the teacher, but questions from the hearers shape the conversation and interchange that happens in the classroom. Good teaching is inherently dialogical.

The monological-versus-dialogical distinction means that there are topics that can and should only be handled in the educational classroom, where feedback can be given, questions asked, and clarifications made. (For example: textual criticism, theodicy, hermeneutics, etc.) This is not possible in the monological situation of a sermon. Thus, the goal and content of preaching should be kept clearly distinct from what can be done through teaching. Preaching and teaching are overlapping but different functions of the pastor's work.

Through our dialogical conversation, my former student came to see the value of what I was advising him. His sermons can be meaty and deep in theological and biblical content—as long as he keeps the mode and ultimate goal in mind when he is writing and delivering his messages. Preaching exhorts and invites.

He came to see that what his church *also* needs is another kind of biblical and theological communication—a separate venue where he and other teachers can address a raft of topics and do so focusing on nuanced explication in a dialogical environment. Kept distinct but working in tandem, preaching and teaching together serve the needs of God's church.

◆ 7 ◆

Encaustic Preaching

Early last year, I took a delightful trip to Santa Fe, New Mexico with my wife, who is a professional artist. Santa Fe is one of the most vibrant art communities in the world, with countless galleries and working studios. Among the many great pieces of art we experienced, I encountered a style of painting I had never seen in person before: encaustic painting.

What is "encaustic" painting? Encaustic refers to a method that uses hot wax colored with pigments and applied in layers. These piled-up layers of melted wax are used to create an image, whether abstract or realistic. Encaustic painting is an ancient technique, and it has created works that have stood the test of time better than most other media. We still have amazing encaustic images created by Greeks in Egypt going back to the second century AD. (Search online for the Fayum mummy portraits.)

The words "caustic" and "encaustic" are related because they both refer to burning. But one is negative, and the other, positive. _Caustic_ burns to destroy (physically or metaphorically). _Encaustic_ burns to create. Encaustic painting heats up wax so that it can be poured and smoothed layer by layer, creating beautiful, multidimensional, luminous pictures. It is a slow art, with each stratum and color cooling before the next is applied.

So what is encaustic preaching? Encaustic preaching as a metaphor casts a vision for taking a long-arc view of preaching, a layer-by-layer, slow approach to your life as a preacher.[8] Preachers should view each sermon they preach as but one layer of wax, one color for one bit of the overall picture. This is how great paintings are made. And it's how great churches are made, too. Consider that in a mere five years, the average preacher will preach over two hundred times. That's two hundred layers of wax poured onto the canvas of your church, shaping and coloring it to create a masterpiece (with the Holy Spirit as the real artist).

Embracing this encaustic vision for preaching relieves pressure to try to do too much in one sermon. It encourages us to let each sermon do its own work, not expecting every thirty-five-minute Sunday morning wax layer to be the whole picture. Each sermon is just one small contribution to your lifework in the pulpit. This is freeing.

Recently I preached on the death of John the Baptist from Matthew 14:1–12. It was an extremely difficult sermon to prepare homiletically and certainly not my best in delivery. But it was a layer. I heated up some wax and poured myself out. I addressed some topics and issues that were unique to that story, some uncommon colors. The sermon provided some particular hues to the painting of our congregation that add to my people's depth and vibrancy. I can take comfort and hope in remembering that I am engaged in a slow art. I can let each sermon be just that—one particular layer—no matter how significant or successful I feel about it.

Encaustic paintings—and I hope you can see some in person sometime—have a physical depth that traditional acrylic and oil paintings don't have. Because they are made up of many layers meticulously added over time, encaustic paintings literally come off the canvas. It can be the same with your preaching. Play the long game. Be content with this week's layer. Let it dry from Monday to Saturday, and then heat up more wax of whatever color your text provides. Then carefully pour it into the lives of your people week after week, layer after layer.

Artistic metaphor

The Preparation
for Preaching

◆ 8 ◆

Manuscript Writing as Thinking

Influenced by your homiletics teachers and ministry mentors, you probably have an ingrained habit of either writing out your sermon as a manuscript or instead using some form of notes. There may also be a difference between what you produce in your study and what you take into the pulpit. Some of you write a full manuscript and then take only an outline with you. Some of you speak from your manuscript. Some of you memorize the whole thing. And some prefer a highly improvised, in-the-moment speaking based on your research and notes.

This variety is an understandable and inevitable function of the great diversity that is humanity itself. Historically and contemporarily, there is no one right method for sermon preparation and delivery. Each preacher needs to find his own way.

But I suggest that there can be great growth in your preaching if you adopt one habit: <u>Manuscript your message</u>.

At some stage in your preparation, write out your sermon in full sentences and paragraphs, regardless of what you use in the pulpit.

The reason is this: Writing is thinking. Putting together sentences and paragraph arguments is *the primary means* by which our thinking is clarified and deepened. Manuscripting your message creates lucidity for you and thereby (potentially) for your hearers—a kind and quality of thinking that can't be had any other way.

Some recent sociolinguistic studies have observed how often we now use computer metaphors to speak (and think) about the human body. We speak of the brain as a computer, accessing memories stored there, with on and off switches, programmed to respond to certain conditions, and so on.

Unfortunately, we have often come to use a bad computer analogy to think of the relationship between writing and thinking. Writing, for many, is simply the monitor's visible manifestation of what is going on in the hard drive of our thinking. In this analogy, writing merely reveals our thoughts.

However, this fails to understand the beautifully complex brain processes that are going on in both writing and thinking. Writing does not merely represent thought processes. *Writing is the means by which thought is created!* It is only through putting words together into sentences and paragraphs that thinking actually occurs. There is no other way.

Annie Dillard wondrously describes it this way:

> When you write, you lay out a line of words. The
> line of words is a miner's pick, a wood-carver's
> gouge, a surgeon's probe. You wield it, and it digs
> a path you follow. Soon you find yourself deep in
> new territory. … The writing has changed, in your
> hands, and in a twinkling, from an expression of
> your notions to an epistemological tool. The new
> place interests you because it is not clear. You
> attend. In your humility, you lay down the words
> carefully, watching all the angles.[9]

Writing takes you from the "expression of your notions to
an epistemological tool." That is, writing is the means to
knowing. The point, then, is that writing is not merely the
byproduct of thinking. Instead, it is the means by which
you can refine and clarify your thinking—in short, truly
understand.

So what does this mean for preachers? It means you
can either do this clarifying and refining thinking *before*
you get into the pulpit—by doing the hard work of writing
your way to understanding—or you can do the first draft
of your thinking in front of an audience. While I definitely
commend creative and spontaneous speaking in preaching,
I suggest that spontaneity and manuscripting are not an
either/or. Instead, take the time and give the effort to force
yourself into thinking-through-writing before Sunday comes.
And then, according to your habits, your desires, and the
Spirit's leading, preach what you've come to understand.

9

Sermon Writing as Sculpture

A few years back, my wife and I had the opportunity to drive around the beautiful North Island of New Zealand. In addition to exploring the stunning scenery, one of our most memorable adventures was serendipitously getting to meet and privately tour the property of one of the Kiwis' most famous sculptors, Terry Stringer. As I reflected later on this remarkable experience and read a bit more about sculpture, it struck me how much writing sermons is like the art of sculpture.[10]

Sculpture—defined as the craft of carving, modeling, or welding material to form a three-dimensional piece of art—is one of the oldest and most enduring forms of human creativity. The process of sculpting involves both blocking and chipping. Blocking, in which one is laying out the image of what the shape and form will eventually be, is the larger planning and envisioning work that takes more time and wrestling. Chipping is the small-scale chiseling, incising, and abrading. Chipping comes by the little hammer blows, bit by bit bringing the shape and form into reality.

This dual process of sculpting describes well the process of good sermon writing. <u>We need to both block and chip our sermons</u>.

When standing before a large piece of marble, a sculptor must have a vision of what the final shape will be, at least generally. As the process unfolds, the sermon writer has the advantage of being able to rearrange paragraphs and chapters; the sculptor, not so much. But in both instances, a general vision, plans for certain lines and cuts, an elbow here, a nose there, are necessary first steps. Blocking in sermon writing is a fluid and flexible process, but it must result in a shape and outline that will guide the actual work of writing.

Sculptors in ancient times often used a technique called "pointing" to produce a copy of another sculpture. Pointing involved building a wooden frame around the original sculpture and using strings to measure the distances between different points on the image. This process enabled one to make an exact copy or a proportionally smaller or larger one.

So too, sermon writers can and should plot out the general shape and relative relationships of points to each other in the piece. Even though we are not merely copying, we should "point" our sermon writing before we embark on its production. For me, this looks like constantly rearranging the sections and moves of a message to find the right flow and structure.

But we also need to do another kind of sermon writing: chipping. Chipping is the minute work. It is the shaping of the earlobe/sentence, the sandaled foot/paragraph. Chipping is the placing of the chisel end on the face of the stone and striking a measured blow. And then doing it again. And then again. And then again. Chipping is the repeated rewriting that will shape a formless rectangle into an elegant arm and beautiful face.

Life is busy and demanding. We often long for more time. And when we do have a block of cherished time, we often waste it. The key to using our sermon-writing time well is to find the proper rhythm between blocking and chipping and to realize that a lot of good sermon writing happens through chipping, not through blocking.

The rhythm is this: We need occasional large blocks of time so that we can lay out the form and shape and direction of our sermon. Blocking times—initial and then periodic— are times given to brainstorming, reading, researching, jotting, outlining, and envisioning.

But then we need short, daily, consistent chipping times. Chipping times focus on the small portions of sermon writing, the paragraph and the section. If we sit down with a manageable chipping goal and simply swing the sentence hammer over and over for a short amount of time, we can produce a lot.

I invite you into the sculptor's studio. Dream, envision, block. Then start chipping and keep chipping. The result may very well be a beautiful marble sermon whose impact may last longer than you.

metaphor of sculptor's studio

◆ 10 ◆

Snack Writing

R ecent studies from the world of nutrition are finding something about eating that is shocking and seems counterintuitive: Snacking throughout the day is better for weight loss and health than eating three square meals. Why? The act of eating and digestion increases our metabolic rate, and therefore, we burn more calories by eating more often. Also, we need energy throughout the day for mental and physical functions, so keeping the nutrients flowing through snacks is far better than stocking up at big meals. The key is to be a strategic snacker. Don't increase your overall calorie intake. Instead, eat a variety of healthy foods throughout the day, and cut the big meals down from three to just two.

There's something here for us in writing sermons in the midst of our busy lives. There may be one in ten thousand preachers whose whole life is dedicated to sermon writing, but for most of us, preparing a sermon is one of many responsibilities we are juggling throughout the week: family, leadership, counseling, relationships, errands, other teaching. As a result, we typically try to carve out some big blocks of time to dedicate to sermon preparation. And this is good. We do need some concentrated, hearty episodes of pondering and reading and writing. Let me suggest, however, that you will be healthier, and your sermons will have greater vigor and vitality, if you introduce strategic snack writing into your weekly schedule.

Every person's diet and needs are a bit different, but here's what sermon snack writing looks like in my life:

- At least a week before I preach a text, I start reading it at least once a day. I try different translations and begin meditating on the passage.

- I start a note file in a note-taking app (I use Evernote) simply titled with the text—for example, "Galatians 5:1–15 Sermon Notes."

- Throughout the week I am conscious of the text, and whenever I think of *anything* that might be related, I take the time right then to add a bullet point in the Evernote file, no matter how large or small. This could be a possible illustration, a possible title, ideas on what a specific phrase or verse might mean, thoughts on structuring the whole sermon, points of application, questions I'm wondering about, anything and everything. There are no bad ideas at this stage!

- About halfway through the week, I sit down and read through several commentaries, making my own notes on things that may prove relevant to my sermon. Depending on my schedule this may take a couple of sessions, but I rarely spend more than an hour at a sitting.

- Near the end of the week, I get more serious and concentrated on fleshing out ideas in note form—either in Evernote or, often, on notepads. I don't use a word-processing document at this point; I want ideas to be free and roaming, not forced into a mold or pattern yet.

- Then, finally, I'm ready for the big meal. For the big meal (usually for me on Saturday), I make myself sit down and type out the first draft of a whole sermon manuscript based on the wide range of notes and ideas I've collected all week. Then I put it aside and come back to it later for a second, smaller meal (early Sunday morning), where I get ruthless with myself—cutting and adding with the urgency of a passionate chef on the opening night of his restaurant.

You have to figure out your own schedule. But the point is that while I do give concentrated "big meal" time to my sermon writing, the vast majority of my preparation is spent in strategic snacking throughout the week. The result is a lot less stress and pressure to be creative and productive in the limited big blocks of time that I have. I can let hors d'oeuvre–sized inspiration strike me throughout the week. My big blocks are the disciplined "eat your vegetables" times that are based in the much more delightful snacking times that I pepper throughout my week. Give it try. Bon appétit!

snacking/dieting metaphor

11

The Rhythm of Education
and the Jigsaw Puzzle

One common mode of biblical preaching uses a classic structure: Introduction, Thesis Statement, Exegesis, Theological Analysis, Application, and Conclusion. Effective as this may be in many times and places, this is not the *only* mode for crafting a sermon. Here are two other metaphors from Ronald Allen—the Rhythm of Education and the Jigsaw Puzzle—each of which provides its own creative insights into the work of sermon writing and delivery.[11]

The Rhythm of Education. The influential twentieth-century thinker Alfred North Whitehead thought and wrote about all kinds of things, from mathematics to metaphysics. He also observed the pattern of how people encounter and interact with a new subject or idea. He describes growth in knowledge (education) as a process or *rhythm* that generally goes through three stages. In the first stage, Romance, people become curious about a topic and begin to think about it with increasing interest and wonder. This is like the beginning of a romance between two people—fascination, magnetism, and the desire to know more. In the second stage, Precision, curiosity leads to comprehension. Questions are answered; interconnections are understood more precisely. In the third stage of education, Generalization, people move to considering how this precise topic connects with the rest of life—patterns are discerned; other areas of life and thought are enriched and deepened by being connected with the new knowledge.

Applied to preaching, this can provide a helpful framework for structuring and crafting the moves of the message. The preacher starts with the Romance stage, inviting hearers indirectly to become intrigued in an idea, helping the topic of the text catch their eye, maybe for the first time. This can often be effectively done with well-honed questions that stimulate interest.

The second move of the sermon is the Precision stage. This is the center of the sermon, in which the preacher works hard to move from initial interest into increasing appreciation and knowledge of the complexity and importance of the text's idea.

Finally, the Generalization stage is analogous to the crucial turn toward application that sermons typically make, though with an emphasis more on how the idea of the sermon connects with other concepts and truths and with life generally. This rhythm of education is a good way to structure a sermon because it is sensitive to how we learn.

The Jigsaw Puzzle. Another approach to conceiving and crafting a sermon comes from considering the analogy of a jigsaw puzzle. Some of our learning happens in a systematic and linear manner, especially when we are being educated in a formal setting—ideas are presented in a lockstep, pyramid manner. But a lot of learning actually happens in a different, more associative way—encountering and connecting bits of data and thoughts that we experience somewhat randomly. This is where the jigsaw puzzle comes in. The experience of putting together a puzzle has some elements of a systematic approach, such as when we separate out the edge pieces first, but for the most part it is a very non-linear process of discovery. When you pick up one of the 1500 pieces of the "Cats Playing with Yarn" or "Boats in the Harbor" picture, you have to examine it, consider it, and then, if possible, connect it with some other piece or pieces that have already found a place. With a complex puzzle, this process takes diligence and patience, but the pleasure of making discoveries and completing the picture is very satisfying.

Applied to preaching, the jigsaw puzzle analogy provides a model for crafting and presenting sermons in a certain way and of a certain kind. Sometimes a text speaks to a complicated issue that has several points and perspectives that must be considered carefully, such as issues of economics, race, gender, or sexuality. Instead of trying to make a simple, linear argument, a jigsaw puzzle approach could free the preacher to recognize and explore this complexity en route to painting a helpful and clear picture. Several different ideas can be held up and examined before putting them together. In this type of sermon, it will likely be best to make three moves: framing the issue (putting the edge pieces together); exploring several distinct issues (examining pieces that may not appear to be connected); and completing the picture (showing how all the pieces fit together).

No single metaphor or approach to sermon writing and delivery excludes the others. There are many helpful ways to conceive of the task of preaching. The Rhythm of Education and Jigsaw Puzzle metaphors provide helpful alternatives to more traditional models, alternatives that may be particularly helpful for certain texts and topics.

Jigsaw puzzle analogy

❖ 12 ❖

Kill Your Darlings

I'll be the first to admit it: "kill your darlings" is a strong and violent statement and not one that would normally be uttered in a book about preaching. But it needs to be a strong statement to communicate the issue at hand.

What little darlings must you kill to grow as a preacher? Your own darling words. Not all of them—I'm not encouraging wordless preaching from the word of God, replacing sermons with mimed skits. But if you want to be an effective preacher, then a lot of the words that you think need to be said and that looked so good and perfect and clever in the first draft of your sermon must be laid aside. (And if your soul resists what I just said, then I guarantee you all the more that you have a lot of little darlings that *must be killed*.)

Why? After all, aren't we wordsmiths? Aren't we called to preach meaty and deep sermons? Yes. But when it comes to preaching content, less is often more. If your goal is to effectively communicate, to persuade, to encourage, to be a life-giving preacher, you probably need to say less than you think you do. Long and wordy sermons are the habit of the immature, not the mature. They are an indicator of laziness in preparation, not skilled labor.

Anne Lamott, a brilliant novelist and author of a great book on writing (*Bird by Bird*), notes that "Every writer you know writes really terrible first drafts, but they keep their butt in the chair. That's the secret of life."[12] The darlings are your hard-produced words. Writing out our thoughts as we prepare to preach is necessary for clarity and persuasive power. But rarely if ever will a first draft be the best and most effective form of those thoughts. The first draft is the building blocks and the scaffolding but not the furnished house of your sermon.

It is necessary to go through a phase of messy construction to get to a livable home. But all of that first-draft messiness must be cleaned up—many little darlings must be killed—if we are going to invite our hearers into the beautiful home of the living word preached.

I have often told young preachers—those especially prone to be wordy and anxious to communicate tons of information—that if they go into the pulpit with eighteen points, guess how many points their congregation will go home with? Zero.

A good sermon will have some distinct moves and a handful of big observations, but too many ideas and too many words will have a counterproductive effect. My mechanic doesn't show me all his tools or explain how brakes work when I need a new A/C compressor. A chef doesn't display the glories of his sixteen-piece whisk collection but chooses the appropriate tool and prepares just the right meal. Your job is to help your hearers stay on the road, to feed them a great meal. A few deep thoughts, picked out of the many that you produced in your study and first draft, developed and illustrated well, can form the greatest gift you could give your congregation.

So what do you do? Be courageous. Pare down your words. Take that sermon manuscript and make fewer points with fewer words, smithed and shaped well. You'll have other sermons to preach. Even if—maybe especially if—you have what seems to be a great turn of phrase or a funny illustration or a side note that you're very passionate about, if it is cluttering up the clarity of your sermon and making it too long and complicated, do yourself and your congregation a favor—kill your darlings.

killing your darling metaphor

13

Iceberg Preaching

Icebergs get a bad rap. Despite being homes for many a polar bear and harbor seal, their primary connotation for the last hundred years has been "Titanic sinking." Fair enough. A destructive floating mountain of packed ice is rather intimidating, especially if you're on a boat in the North Atlantic.

Connecting icebergs with preaching likewise may not be a very positive thought. Anything icy and cold will especially have negative connotations when connected to sermonizing. "Iceberg preaching" may sound like advice to crush people with the cold weight of doctrine or moralism.

Instead, I'd like to suggest that these glacier-born floating islands of fresh water have something to teach us about the life of preaching when we consider how icebergs are shaped. Icebergs help us think about sermons in terms of ballast and gravitas.

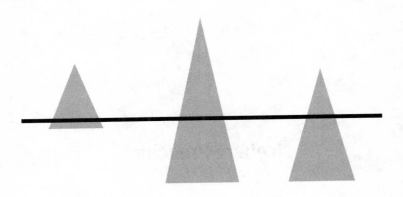

To explain, let's consider three representations of what an iceberg could look like.

In the first triangle above, the visible part above the water line forms almost the entirety of the iceberg. In the middle triangle, the underwater part is roughly equal to what is seen above the water. In the third triangle—the one that most closely represents the actual shape of Arctic icebergs—what lies underwater is the bulk of the iceberg's mass while the visible tip is relatively small. It is this third shape that makes attempting to navigate through berg-filled waters particularly precarious, as we know from that famous voyage of 1912.

How do these images relate to the life of preaching? Each pictures the relationship between the preacher and the sermon in a different way. The water line represents the division between the public and the private, the interior of the preacher and the exterior:

- In the first image, the sermon represents all that
  the preacher is and knows. His knowledge is
  limited biblically, theologically, and experien-
  tially. The sermon and the preacher's knowledge are coextensive. The sermon is a pastiche
  of platitudes and quotes from other people.

- In the middle image, the sermon and the under-
  lying knowledge are both large. This knowledge
  is rooted in a depth of learning. The height of
  the tip is possible because of the years of the
  packed ice of insight under the surface. The
  sermon is complex, laying out six points, each
  with four subpoints and references to three different scholarly opinions.

- In the third image, the sermon feels accessible but has an unseen depth and stability. This
  sermon leaves hearers with a clear idea of what
  was being said and a heart that is searching and
  wondering.

Our preaching lives should look like the third picture, a
true image of an iceberg. Every analogy breaks down at
some point, of course, and I'm not suggesting good preaching should contain hidden jagged edges that will trick and
sink people. Quite the opposite—the point is that only the
third image combines what is needed for a life of effective

preaching: *simplicity in preaching that is rooted in depth of understanding.*

The unseen portion of our preaching provides ballast and gravitas, a felt weightiness and meaningfulness that is lacking in the first image. At the same time, this bulk does not appear on the surface of the sermon. When a sermon is too heavy above the water line, the result is not greater effectiveness but lesser.

A great sermon is simple and clear, based in complexity and depth. Simplicity without depth will float aimlessly and deteriorate. Complexity without clarity reflects immaturity. Simple clarity rooted in iceberg-sized knowledge and experience makes a powerful and hospitable mountain.

So how do you become an iceberg preacher? On the "below the water" side of things, give yourself to study and learning, both formal and informal. Don't be content with surface knowledge of an issue, even if it is the right answer and will please your audience. Cultivate a mind and soul that are curious and awake, always learning, always seeking, always working on your craft. If you have settled into going through the motions and are no longer learning as a preacher, it is time to retire or get a different job.

On the "above the water" level—the actual preaching of the sermon—labor hard to make your messages simple and clear. Don't be content with dumping on your people the in-depth data of your learning. Overly complex sermons reveal laziness, not intelligence. There should be a strong filter standing between your study and your pulpit, with most of what you know strained out and refined into a clear and pure message.

We should want to shape our sermons like beautiful water-mountains that have a deep and hidden ballast. This is iceberg preaching.

Iceberg metaphor

◆ 14 ◆

"This Sermon Stinks"

I can hardly remember a Saturday night in my first fifteen years of preaching (and several times since) when I didn't experience the despairing and overwhelming feeling that "This Sermon Stinks" (TSS).

Sometimes it was more devastating than others, but I always was afflicted with this sense to some degree. I think on the rare occasion that I *didn't* experience TSS on Saturday, my sermon was not very good on Sunday. I came to understand that TSS was inevitable—and I'd rather have it happen on Saturday afternoon, when there was still time to do something about it, than on Sunday afternoon, when there wasn't!

As I have reflected on this phenomenon, a couple of important questions have challenged me:

1. Why did I so often experience TSS? and

2. What is the relationship, if any, of TSS to a good sermon?

The answer to the first question took a long time to come to me, and it arrived through a side door. As director of the PhD program at our school, I teach a class to all new students on the life of the scholar, including the challenges of academic writing. This has given me the opportunity to reflect on my own struggles to write consistently. At the same time, my wife, who is a professional mosaic artist, has been on her own journey of understanding the typical artist's struggles with producing pieces of art. All of these struggles and experiences came together when I learned about the six steps of the creative process. Here they are:

1. This is awesome.

2. This is tricky.

3. This stinks.

4. I stink.

5. This might be okay.

6. This is awesome.

These six somewhat comical steps describe the U-shaped graph of the emotional experience of anyone who is engaged in creating something. Interest and potential is there at the beginning (Step 1), but as you begin to work on something, you realize it is more difficult than you thought (Step 2), and then what you have attempted to create isn't that good really (Step 3), leading you to despair and to question your own value and ability (Step 4). It is incredibly easy to quit at this point, and every artist and writer has stacks of unfinished projects that got derailed at this step—sometimes rightly so, but sometimes not. But if you keep pressing on and refining, you can begin to find your footing again (Step 5) and eventually produce something that, if not always exactly "awesome," is at least something worth making (Step 6).

This articulation of what I had been experiencing in sermon writing—which is a creative act, whether or not you've realized that before—was incredibly life giving because I finally understood *why* I so often experienced the discouraging TSS in sermon preaching. TSS is the inevitable Steps 3 and 4 of the creative process.

And this answers the second, related question: What is the relationship of TSS to a good sermon? The answer to this became obvious in both experience and concept. TSS is truly inevitable if you want to produce good work because creative work is a process of struggle toward the good. As frustrating as TSS is, without it you can't really produce anything of substance, as all writers and artists and other types of creators can testify.

So what does this mean as a small step toward better preaching? Simply—well, not so simply because it is emotionally difficult—embrace the creative process. Don't resent the weekly TSS journey. The painful up-down-up of the process is the necessary hot fire that refines the impure mixed metal of your ideas into pure silver that can be crafted into a fine setting for the gospel diamond. TSS will never completely go away, but it does get easier over the years, especially as you come to understand what is happening. Expect and embrace the process. Count it as the price you must pay to be used by God, the deep and secret gift you give to your congregation each week. ⌡

The Practice
of Preaching

✦ 15 ✦

The First Minute of a Sermon

A ll of us have enjoyed the diverse and wild-west world of YouTube. There is a video for everything, whether you want to learn to flush the heater core on a 2004 Mazda RX8, understand the difference between baroque and classical cellos, or watch Bad Lip Reading versions of the NFL, to name just a few of my own recent viewings.

I've recently seen another side of YouTube as the producer of a show.[13] The "backside" of YouTube is their powerful "video analytics" mode that shows stunningly detailed data to the people who create and upload videos. I won't scare you with the creepiness of how much they know about you demographically when you click on a video, but I will note this one interesting thing I've learned: most people make a snap decision within a few seconds about whether they are going to keep watching. Then, other mental windows of interest begin to close as time ticks along. If you and I aren't immediately hooked by a particular video—either because of its quality, perceived lack of relevance, or something that turned us off—very rarely will we give it even a full minute of our time.

This is because the human brain has the huge and tiring job of analyzing the countless signals it is receiving from our neural network. Our brains have to make choices about what they will pay attention to. Things that don't make sense, are irrelevant, or are poorly done will generally be judged, ignored, and forgotten. And all of this happens within seconds.

Now some may offer loud laments about the decreased attention spans of the younger generation (whippersnappers!), and it is true that the quick-fix mode of screen-based technologies can decrease our attentiveness. But we are talking here about something that is more than generational; it is biological.

If you're still reading, then I've done a decent job of what I want you to take away from this essay. What I've written took less than a minute for you to read. If you're still with me, then I must have said enough interesting, relevant, and comprehensible things for you to keep reading.

Here is why all this matters. That first minute of your sermon is absolutely crucial to your homiletical effectiveness. Yes, different people have different attention spans. Yes, some people will listen to you diligently and carefully even if your first minute isn't very engaging. Yes, some people will be distracted or apathetic regardless of how well-crafted your first minute is. Yes, ultimately the Holy Spirit can do whatever he wants through the preaching of the word.

But with all those qualifications in place, <u>we can still rec-ognize that from a rhetorical, homiletical, pedagogical, and neurological perspective—let's just say it, a *human* perspec-tive—that first minute of your sermon matters a lot.</u> It is your responsibility as a preacher to craft the opening of your sermon with intentionality to grab and keep the attention of the easily distracted people hearing your voice. Here are some first-minute Don'ts and Dos.

Don't:

- Step into the pulpit ill-prepared for the physical part of your work: check before the service starts that your mic works and the podium is the right height, that you know what the lights will look like in your eyes and on your manuscript when you are speaking, etc. Eliminate distractions that will hinder your homiletic opening.

- Start with time- and attention-wasting activities like turning on your mic, taking off your watch, drinking water—do all these things before you step into place or don't do them at all.

- Start with self-deferential remarks—how you're not that great of a preacher or not as good as some-one else. Not only are these counterproductive to your goal and calling in preaching, they are also almost certainly coming from insecurity hoping to be placated, not from a place of wisdom and strength.

- Start by talking about anything other than your sermon. Often guest speakers waste precious time thanking and praising their hosts. We get it. We don't need it. Start preaching.

- Demean your audience in any way. Adult learners will quickly withdraw from active participation if they are offended. Their windows will close.

Do:

- Start preaching immediately.

- Write out and memorize or nearly memorize your opening paragraphs. Your first words are vitally important, so craft them well and know them so you can be present and engage your audience by looking at them. And smile.

- Often start with a thoughtful question, one that engages the hearers' minds in a genuine way. (See also chapter 19, "The Power of Predictions.")

- Often start with something humorous, intriguing, and/or personal. People are (usually unconsciously) deciding whether they like you, whether they can trust you, whether they want to listen to you. All the things you do in the first minute will contribute to that judgment and therefore to whether they will be open to the word of God that you are there to present.

So take the small step of working hard on that first minute of your sermon. This small investment pays big dividends.

16

The Last Minute of a Sermon

"Better is the end of a thing than its beginning," quips the somewhat cynical sage of Ecclesiastes (7:8). Homileticians and rhetoricians would agree—at least in part. *Both* the beginning of a sermon and its end are the most important parts in terms of impact and memorability. We know that of the roughly three to four thousand words in a thirty-five-minute sermon, the average brain will only imbibe a small percentage in a lasting way. Vivid illustrations and personal stories have a good shot. What you say in the first and last minutes of your sermon have prime opportunity. Most of the rest of it will be forgotten. So paying attention to that last minute really matters.

Different preachers will have varying philosophies and habits regarding how much they plan out and write out what they are going to say in the sermon—from complete manuscripts to only jotted-down main points. That's okay. But all preachers should be thoughtful, planned, and intentional with how they spend the precious currency of the last minute of the sermon. In addition to not waiting until the last minute to think about your last minute, here are some last-minute Don'ts and Dos for your message:

Don't:

- Fail to land the plane. There are few worse ways to ruin an otherwise good sermon than by petering out—ending weakly, with no clarity, no finality. I've actually heard a preacher end with "Well, that's all I've got to say." A sermon is not a casual conversation. It is an intentionally crafted communicative experience. Don't fly around with your sermon until you run out of gas and then crash. Land the plane with fuel in the tank and passenger safety in mind by knowing where you want to end. Then do it.

- Surprise your hearers that your message is over. They should receive verbal and non-verbal clues as you are coming to the end. Tell your hearers that you're nearing the end by giving them a numbered list of how many application points there are or by using expressions like "Finally" or "So to wrap this all up." (That is, as long as you really are close to ending! Don't say these things with ten minutes left. I've been guilty of this, as my wife and kids have pointed out before.)

- Introduce new ideas or new arguments in the last minute. You may want to use a new, final illustration, though make sure it doesn't take the sermon in a whole different direction. This can be distracting and stimulate thoughts that don't help hearers feel the end. It's better in that last minute to reiterate what you've been saying and point people to God in Christ with familiar clarity and life-giving hope.

✱ • Conclude your sermon with a "prayer" that isn't really speaking to God but is instead reiterating your three points to the congregation. "Lord, help these people remember that (1) We should..." This is neither good prayer nor good preaching.

Do:

- Remember that every sermon is a story, and so the ending should be as crafted and intentional as the beginning. (See chapter 20, "Every Sermon a Story.")

- Go for the heart in very specific applications. Don't be content with general and abstract platitudes. I often spend the last five to seven minutes of a sermon applying my point to the real-life situations of teenagers, young marrieds, retired people, the apathetic, the joyful, the depressed, the broken, or those facing chronic pain.

- Write out your ending. As with the first minute of your message, the last minute is essential in terms of overall impact, so don't leave it to chance and laziness. Be intentional and write out what you are going to say, paying attention to the content, shape, and quality of your words.

- End on a positive, inviting note. If you end with a negative word, the congregation will exit the sanctuary glad the sermon is over and leave it there, not in their hearts and minds, fleeing its discomfort.

- Tie the point of the whole message together. Your big idea—in content and application—should be the last thing they leave with. Over lunch they should be able to repeat to each other what the point of your sermon was. The last minute is the best place to implant that in their hearts and minds.

You are reading the last few sentences of this essay because endings matter. So take the small preaching step of ending your sermons well.

◆ 17 ◆

Preaching the Church Calendar

Humans have been devising ways to keep track of time as far back as we know, from megalithic structures like Stonehenge, through Chinese, Persian, and Roman clock mechanisms, all the way down to one's choice between the "Classic Muscle Cars" and "Kittens in Baskets" calendars at the Christmastime mall kiosk.

Today, there are diverse ways we organize our calendar, each of which frames our experience of time in particular ways. We have the school year, complete with back-to-school sales, breaks for holidays, and graduations. We have the fiscal year, with companies and other organizations tracking finances by quarters and ending and beginning new budget cycles, often in July. We have various holidays, many of which involve travel to see family or trips to certain tourist destinations. All of these are rooted in the cultures and subcultures in which they are practiced. Starting classes in August would seem as weird to an Australian schoolgirl as going to Disney World over Easter break would to an Afghan.

We see throughout the Bible that God's people were directed to organize their time by recognizing and celebrating special times and seasons and holy days (whence our word "holiday"). For example, on the fourteenth and fifteenth days of the month Nisan, the Passover was celebrated, remembering God's deliverance of the people from slavery in Egypt. In the month of Tishrei are the very important holidays Yom Kippur (the Day of Atonement) and Sukkot (the Feast of Tabernacles). Later Jewish festivals include Purim on 14 Adar, remembering the story of Esther, and Hanukkah on 25 Kislev, celebrating the rededication of the temple in 164 BC. And of course, set by the pattern of creation itself, God established one day out of seven to be a sabbath, a day of rest that is different from the other days of work.

How does all of this relate to our lives as preachers? Following this biblical and universal human pattern of time and season observance, the church from its early days has recognized different days and seasons to organize our lives. Eventually this developed into a complex and beautiful church calendar. While this church calendar is not a new law that must be observed as part of the Christ covenant (see Galatians 4:10; Colossians 2:16), the church has long recognized the value and benefit of organizing our Christian lives around the story of Christ. The church calendar provides a rhythm of life that is intended to remind believers about the saving work of God in Christ and to guide and shape the sensibilities and affections of Christians.]

The seasons of the year mark different parts of Jesus' story: the foretelling and birth (Advent), the time of suffering and death (Lent), the time of resurrection (Easter), the time of the giving of the Spirit (Pentecost). Between these specific seasons there is also "Ordinary Time," and throughout the year, specific Sundays honor different historical and theological truths about Christianity (Trinity Sunday, The Baptism of the Lord Sunday, etc.). Whether we come from a high- or low-church tradition, we all can recognize that there are benefits to observing special days. After all, nearly all Christians have always met on Sundays (rather than another random day of the week) to commemorate the day Jesus rose from the dead. Likewise, Christians regularly observe at the very least the special days of Easter and Christmas.

The point for our preaching and our church lives is this: Regardless of your past practices, consider the benefits of weaving into the preaching schedule certain church calendar practices. These are designed to help believers remember and commemorate their identity as Christians. The no-brainers that most people are already celebrating are Christmas, Good Friday, and Easter. The next small step for some would be the four Sundays of Advent (a time of preparation before Christmas) and Maundy Thursday (the Last Supper and Jesus' washing of the disciples' feet). It is also beneficial to include Lent (a somber season of preparation for Easter), Pentecost Sunday, Trinity Sunday, and Epiphany (the twelfth day of Christmas commemorating the coming of the magi).

Observance of these special days and seasons is no threat to regular preaching through books of the Bible, a particularly strong emphasis in most evangelical traditions. Preaching certain texts on special days can be a good discipline and can also provide a helpful reminder of core biblical truths and the story of Jesus in the midst of whatever other sermon series is going on. Additionally, if you don't want to give the whole sermon to a particular holiday, you can use other aspects of the worship service—readings, prayers, confessions, and so on—to highlight special Sundays and seasons. Churches are free to adopt as little or as much of the church calendar as they desire, meeting people where they are and taking them to the next step according to local and denominational customs. ⌐In all, the calendar is a gift that helps to reshape our sensibilities and redirect our hearts toward God's presence in the world through Christ. ⌡

◆ 18 ◆

Preaching the Cultural Calendar

Whether we interpret it as merely fun or, cynically, as sheer crass marketing, we now have a "National Day of … " for just about everything. Whether or not you know it, today just may very well be National Blueberry Pancake Day, National Bubble Wrap Appreciation Day, National Law Enforcement Day, National Cream Puff Day, or National Dress Up Your Pet Day (a few from January alone).

Likely, none of these examples will affect what you preach or how you plan a Sunday service. But other special days that are part of one's culture do weave their way into what happens in church—by either unexamined tradition, outside pressure, or pastoral intentionality.. Should you preach a dedicated sermon that relates to special days such as Mother's Day, Father's Day, or Thanksgiving? What about Sanctity of Life Sunday, Martin Luther King Jr. Day, Adoption Sunday, or Sunday for the Persecuted Church? How about Veteran's Day, Memorial Day, Independence

Day, or Labor Day (perhaps with Matthew 20:1–16 as your text)?

There is no clear right or wrong answer, but decisions must be made with wisdom that is sensitive to one's own subculture and local and denominational church traditions. We need not argue in absolute terms either for or against the inclusion of a certain special Sunday. These are matters of *adiaphora* (matters not essential to the faith). But we do need intentionality. Extremes on either side should be avoided; there is no badge of self-righteous honor to be earned by completely ignoring the cultural calendar, nor should it be assumed that because a particular holiday has been honored, it should continue to be so and in the same way. Pastors and church leaders should think about which Sundays they want to observe and why, explaining their decisions to their congregations as necessary.

What are the pros and cons of celebrating a particular special Sunday? One con is that if a church honors certain Sundays, this can end up consuming much of the church's calendar, especially if the church is also using aspects of the church year calendar (see chapter 17, "Preaching the Church Calendar"). If a church is dedicated to *lectio continua*, wherein books of the Bible are preached through in sequence, too many special Sundays can disrupt the valuable continuity of this practice. Practically as well, if a church sets aside a number of special Sundays, some congregants may begin to lobby for the inclusion of a Sunday that is special to them. "You had Veteran's Day, why not Memorial Day?" "You observed Sanctity of Life Sunday, why not a Sunday for racial reconciliation?" I understand that a pastor may find it easier to observe no special Sundays so as to avoid this potentially uncomfortable and conflictual situation.

However, there are reasons to honor special Sundays that are worth considering. It is good and appropriate to occasionally preach topical or theological sermons, even if one's church is dedicated to biblical exposition as the primary homiletical mode. The church's history testifies to the regular inclusion of sermons that help people understand big and important truths that require a whole-Bible understanding. So thinking about motherhood, fatherhood, parenting, issues of death and remembering, even questions of war and national identity—these are all good and appropriate uses of the sermon. Closely related is that preaching and the Bible are meant to be applicable to all of life, helping people learn to think and live biblically. Paying attention to what certain Sundays highlight provides a prime opportunity to instruct and shape our hearers. It is also good and appropriate within God's kingdom to give honor where honor is due and extend encouragement to those in need—whether they be veterans, mothers, other ethnicities, or those suffering for the faith.

Handling some special Sundays well requires a wise and sensitive spirit. The current generation is more sensitive than in the past to the widespread and painful experience of infertility. However, this does not mean that Mother's Day should be avoided or apologized for—mothers are still worthy of honor even if not every woman is able to be a mother. The pastor should be aware of the mixed emotions in the congregation and wisely speak to both sides.

Granted, there are lots of bad fathers that have scarred their children, and some in our congregations are orphans. But fathers also need encouragement and exhortation, and the fatherhood of God is a central biblical theme, worthy of highlighting.

Some congregants (especially those under thirty) may be hypersensitive to an aggressive nationalism—rightly so—but those who have served as veterans and who have given their lives in service of country are still worthy of honoring and remembering.

In all of this, the key is wisdom. For any particular special Sunday, one solution is to use other aspects of the worship service instead of the sermon to note the occasion. Use a prayer, reading, or moment of recognition that honors the special cultural Sunday while conducting the rest of the service as normal.

◆ 19 ◆

The Power of Predictions

What do you think I am going to argue in this essay? What is it about our brains that makes question asking so important?

What good do you think asking questions in your sermons might do?

"I see what you did there" might be your reaction right now. That's ok. I am beginning this essay by asking you questions that invite you to predict answers. I'm doing this because there is great power in predictive questions. And that's what I'm going to argue—one small way to greatly improve the effectiveness of your sermons is to <u>ask thoughtful, stimulating predictive questions.</u>

Now let's back up a little bit. In James Lang's delightful book *Small Teaching* (see the Introduction), he surveys several studies conducted by education and learning specialists regarding the power of prediction. The idea—backed by impressive stats—is that when students are invited to predict answers to questions about material they are about to learn, their comprehension and retention is significantly enhanced. For example, students who are given a pre-test before being presented with completely unfamiliar material in a Music Appreciation class end up performing significantly better on later tests than those who do not take the pre-test. Or another example: In a literature class, students who are asked halfway through their reading of *Moby-Dick* to guess what will come next and how characters will behave will grasp and engage the story much more deeply.

Why does the cognitive act of prediction deepen learning? As Lang points out, our brains do not store information in a file-folder kind of system, in which knowledge is simply kept and retrieved in isolated packets. Quite the opposite: Our brains function more like nets, with a network of interconnected ideas, concepts, facts, and experiences. Knowledge is the "web of connections we have between things we know."[14] When we make attempts at prediction, our minds naturally seek connections with what we know and have experienced that will help us guess what may happen next. This activity stimulates the brain to make new connections, thickening the neural network. That's what we call *learning*.

So what does this have to do with our preaching? You've probably already predicted what the straightforward application is: Learn to ask thoughtful questions that invite your hearers to ponder and anticipate what you're discussing. This can take many forms. I sometimes begin a sermon with a question that asks my parishioners to consider what they would do in a certain situation. Or when working the argument of a Pauline text, I will pause and ask, "What in the world is God going to say next?" Or when retelling a powerful biblical narrative, I will pause at the high point of the story and say, "What do you think is going to happen?"

These kinds of predictive questions engage our hearers powerfully, grabbing their attention or re-grabbing it when it has wandered into thoughts about what's for lunch or what they should wear to work tomorrow. This technique is a little bit of homiletical wisdom based on the beautiful way God has made our mysterious minds. Do you think it could work?

❖ 20 ❖

Every Sermon a Story

Through and through, we are story creatures. We do not exist nor can we conceive of our lives apart from a narrative timeline. Our past, our present, and our future describe our existence and identity. God, who alone is timeless, set us into this four-dimensional reality, and therefore it is no accident that the vast majority of Holy Scripture consists of stories. Moreover, even the 20 percent or so of the Bible that is not directly narrative in form only makes sense when situated into the Bible's grand story that runs from creation in Genesis to new creation in Revelation.

This pervasive creaturely narrative reality in both life and Scripture means something for our preaching: The most effective sermons are those that tap into this deeply buried human and biblical story river. Sermons from any part of Scripture and on any topic can and should tell a story, not to be cutesy or merely relevant but because story-bound is who we are as God's creatures.

So what does this look like? Consider the basic structure of every story. Thankfully, we don't have to start from
scratch. Going back at least to Aristotle, what ancient thinkers observed, and what we still find helpful, is that stories
develop across the mental timeline of a *plot*. Unlike arguments, which proceed stepwise from proposition to conclusion, every story is built on the same roller-coaster template
of plot development. And central to plot is some tension
or problem that is presented, developed, and then resolved.
Without tension there is no story.

The plotline pattern of every story—whether it is a trag-
edy, a romantic comedy, a journey, or a human development
tale—can be illustrated as follows.

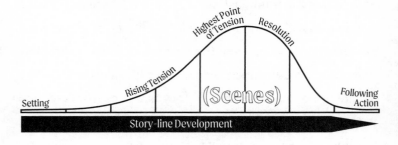

Setting. Rising Tension. Highest Point of Tension. Resolution.
Following Action.[15] This is every story's structure. It should
also be every sermon's framework. God has embedded our
lives in story, and therefore, it is stories above all else that
engage our whole person—body, mind, and heart.

So again, what does this look like? Whether you are
preaching from an Old Testament prophet, a New Testament

epistle, the narratives of the history of David, or the Gospel biographies of the Son of David, the structure of your sermon should be built upon the scaffolding of this basic plotline framework.

Setting. The introduction to your sermon sets the tone and mental space for what is about to occur. The first words out of your mouth matter as much as the first line of a novel or the "once upon a time" of a mythic epic. In your Setting you should introduce the idea your message is going to address.

Rising tension. Very soon in your introduction (I aim for within the first two minutes), you need to raise some question, some tension, some issue that engages your hearers. Maybe it is a question or emotional struggle or frustration that is well known already. Or maybe you will raise a question they've never really articulated before. Either way, this is a crucial stage in engaging your hearers. With no plot, there is no story. With no tension, there is no sermon.

High point of tension. Your sermon should reach a mountaintop of tension. People should feel the height and depth of what you're talking about as you bring the ideas of the text to a palpable point of need and intensity. A story that never changes tone is boring. So too a sermon.

Resolution. Your sermon is not designed to create anxiety or burden souls with some unresolvable dilemma. The key to the sermon both rhetorically and theologically is the biblical resolution that the text provides for the tension it (and you) has highlighted. In some sermons, the resolution happens relatively early, and the bulk of the sermon unpacks the resolution. In other sermons, the tension builds until the penultimate move.

Following action. In narratives, the following action is typically implicit more than explicit; the story may tell what happened to the characters for good or for bad, but only pedantic stories get overly "preachy" at the end (think Ayn Rand). Sermons, however, should work hard at kindly and lovingly applying the resolved tension of the text to people's real, twenty-first-century lives. Explicit and specific application is exactly what people want and need and what we are called to offer.

As with any engaging story, you shouldn't explicitly explain this plotline framework in your sermon. But it should be there in your sermon building. The studs and electrical wiring of the sermon's plot structure will be covered with a nicely painted wall of words. But the structure should be behind those walls as you create a beautiful and livable world for your hearers to inhabit. Make every sermon a story, no matter what kind of text you are preaching.

metaphor of story

21

Make Music in Your Sermon

There's nothing quite like live music. The technology that enables us to record music and hear it anytime is an amazing gift, but it is another thing altogether to see skilled musicians perform in the flesh, in real time. Something happens that is more than the songs. The embodied and shared moment matters. And even more, sometimes there are shared embodied moments that border on the transcendent: that jam session or concert where a mysterious combination of musicians, music, hearers, and space adds up to more than the sum of its parts. Truly magical.

Yet musicians are real people, and this means that sometimes the making of music falls into the rut of roteness, going through the motions of the chord progressions, lyrics, or arpeggios. This is a particularly acute problem for the professionals, that tiny minority of musicians who actually make a living *as* musicians. Repetition brings numbness as familiarity breeds contempt.

So too, every sermon is a live, embodied, shared creation offered by that tiny minority of people who actually make a living studying Holy Scripture and teaching it to others. And the rut of roteness is always drawing us into its furrow too, regardless of our skills, efforts, and desires to be faithful and true.

I have seen a lot of live music of all genres and flavors. But at the top of my list was a concert I attended in recent years by a group of highly skilled jazz musicians called Postmodern Jukebox. What made this concert so memorable was that they were not just *performing their songs*; they were *making music*. That is, it was apparent they were not just going through the motions of playing the right notes with excellence. They were present, in the moment, on the edge, creating music right in front of us, with all its risks and wholehearted, full-throated joy.

This difference—performing songs versus making music—should be a vision that drives and shapes our preaching. The skills and labor must be present in both preparation and the pulpit, but we should never be content with that. We must not think that our work is done if we've played the right sermonic notes and scales. People need more than a performance—they can download anyone's sermons—they need us to create music for them each week, live and alive.

How do we do this? For our part, we consciously make ourselves present and ready to take some risks: to be vulnerable, passionate, humble, all in, and to not hold back in self-protection or fear of failure. Right before I step in front of the congregation, I always remind myself that what I'm doing matters in ways far beyond my own performance and skills. This preaching moment is God at work for good in the world—changing the direction of a young person's life, healing a marriage, giving hope in the midst of a cancer trial. This helps me show up wholeheartedly.

Ultimately, though, that mysterious, transcendent musical moment is out of our control. It is the work of God himself through the Holy Spirit. This is why we gladly pray for God to do the work. And that is good news. Show up each Sunday morning as a skilled musician ready to play the instrument through which God will sing to his beloved people. Reject approaching the sermon and Sunday as merely a skilled performance, and instead ask God to make music through you.

music metaphor

22

Always Exposition?

You may have a negative reaction to what I'm about to say, so try to understand before you disagree. Here we go: I'm not sure that we should expositionally preach every part of the Bible. There, I said it. Take a deep breath and let me explain what I mean.

I know the first objection to my claim can and should be 2 Timothy 3:16–17:

> All Scripture is God-breathed and is useful for teaching, rebuking, correcting and training in righteousness, so that the servant of God may be thoroughly equipped for every good work.

This important text is not only making a statement about the nature of Holy Scripture; it also states what the function and goal of God's word is: to teach, rebuke, and train for the purpose of transforming people in virtuous behavior. These verses and this idea have been important to all of Christianity from its beginning, but maybe especially in the Protestant tradition, and maybe doubly-especially in the evangelical sub-tradition, which puts an extremely high value on the *preaching* of the word as the main means of gospel ministry. As a result, a distinguishing identity marker for many modern evangelicals is expositional preaching from the Bible. That is, evangelicals don't want to just dip into the Bible to construct ideas or teachings, but rather, they wish to give a systematic explanation of what the Bible says. Historically this has been called *lectio continua*. A badge of honor is often the preaching of whole books of the Bible (often taking multiple years to explain a letter that can be read aloud in twenty minutes).

I realize to suggest that maybe we needn't preach expositionally from every portion of the Bible is going against a long homiletical habit. But I'd ask you to consider a few thoughts.

To begin with, saying that all of Holy Scripture is useful for teaching, rebuking, and training is not the same thing as saying that all of Scripture must be handled and used in the same way. Yes, all of Scripture is inspired and profitable and useful, but we must consider how it is meant to function toward these ends. For example, the Psalms are prayers and songs to be sung. We can and do learn theology and truth from them, and thus they are profitable and useful, *but we learn from them by using them according to their purpose*—as personal and corporate prayers and songs.

Continuing along this line of thought, we can also consider another portion of Holy Scripture, the book of Proverbs. Shall we preach this expositionally? As soon as you try, if you are going to be sensitive to how the book is structured and functions, you will quickly realize that you need another strategy besides proceeding verse by verse—something topical at best. It's certainly fine and good to preach topical sermons from Proverbs. But what if the profitable point of Proverbs is for personal memorization and application more than exposition? They should be taught so that people can understand them, but maybe preaching through the book isn't the best way to do so. Was Proverbs put together with the intent of being exposited in sermons? It seems clearly not.

Or to press the matter in a slightly different direction, take a book like the letter to the Galatians. (Now we're cutting close to the Protestant bone!) This whole letter has one big and passionate point: that requiring Jewish practices and obedience to the Law as part of the Christian faith is a corruption of the gospel. It's pretty easy to see this is Paul's point because he says it over and over and over again with various illustrations and arguments. When you try to preach through Galatians, you soon realize that, even taking ten to twelve verses each week, you're going to have eight or nine messages in the middle of the book that are literally the same argument on repeat.

I realize the super-pious among us may respond, "Well, it's God's word and he must want us to say it that many times!"

I get that. But might I suggest that the power of this message comes precisely through experiencing it in *short sequence*? The powerful punch is the fast-action barrage of Paul's passionate plea, repeating himself with multiple illustrations in short order. It is the rhetorical repetition taken all at once that communicates the message most clearly and forcefully. Instead of preaching nine weeks of the same message, what if we preached five total messages from Galatians, taking together the larger portions that repeat the same argument?

We could consider other examples—Job, Ecclesiastes, Acts—and ponder the ways in which they are useful and fruitful for training but also see that maybe the way this happens best is through experiencing and using these texts according to their form (personally and corporately) rather than through expositing them verse by verse in a sermon.

Really what I'm suggesting here is <u>a simple extension</u> of <u>the important idea of interpreting texts according to their</u> <u>genres</u>. So I'd ask you to consider that in our desire to honor Holy Scripture and learn from God, valuing the bold preaching of the word, ironically we may misuse and miss the way different portions of Scripture are profitable and useful. All Scripture is profitable and does teach us, but the way we use and teach from various portions of the Bible should vary according to how each text is meant to function—some in direct teaching, some in leading us how to sing or pray, and some in giving us memorizable, pithy sayings to guide our lives.

◆ 23 ◆

The Unexamined Sermon Is Not Worth Preaching

When Socrates was tried by his fellow Athenians for corrupting the youth of the city, he refused to stop seeking and speaking the truth because, he proclaimed, "The unexamined life is not worth living." As a riff on these famous words, I suggest that as painful as it may be for us, an unexamined sermon is not worth preaching.

This means you will need to regularly seek out intentional and meaningful evaluation of your preaching by others, uncomfortable as it may be. You need to systematically and intentionally pursue the "examined life" for your preaching ministry. Every sermon and every preacher has room for at least *some* improvement, and sometimes that room is mansion sized.

Why you may not want to do this. Systematic and intentional evaluation of your preaching is a scary prospect. Fear of giving voice to congregational criticisms is understandable.

Some of these criticisms are justified, and you may not want to face them, like that knocking noise in the engine of your minivan that sounds expensive. It's much easier to just turn up the radio. Some of these criticisms are completely unjustified, the grumbling of the frozen chosen who are extremely confident in their own narrow and negative opinions. You may think it is unhelpful to give oxygen and space to these choking weeds. As Harry S. Truman said, "How far would Moses have gone if he had taken a poll in Egypt?"

Why you should do this. Despite these fears, there are many positive and far weightier reasons for intentionally seeking out sermon evaluation. Good leaders in every field are constantly evaluating and being evaluated. In business, in organizations, and personally, *some* growth can happen unintentionally for a time, but eventually, entropy is the rule. Things deteriorate. They don't get better naturally. Additionally, even high performers need to go back to the basics sometimes. When the skilled basketball team loses a big game (or almost does) because of missed free throws and lack of hustle, the next practice is going to involve cardio conditioning and strict shooting drills—back to the basics to go forward.

In addition to being good for your own growth, intentional evaluation of the church's preaching helps the preacher and everyone else to remember how the body of Christ functions. The called preacher does have a special and especially visible role, but it is not as king or dictator or CEO or

privileged heir. The preacher is the one whose role is to teach
and exhort. Even as we rightly evaluate and seek improvement in every other ministry area to keep the body healthy,
so too we need to regularly evaluate the preaching ministry.

How you should do this. I hope that you are at least open
to this potentially scary prospect. How should we go about
it practically? What you do to implement evaluation is crucial to its effectiveness and value. Here are some suggestions:

- Create a form to guide questions of evaluation.
  Include questions about both delivery and con-
  tent. What was effective? What was helpful?
  When did you get lost in listening to the sermon?

- Start the habit of regular evaluation conducted
  by the other pastoral staff. Weekly or biweekly
  is ideal. The key is for the preacher to not be
  defensive but instead to create a safe environment behind closed doors where the staff can
  give honest feedback. I know of several churches
  that have created a culture of examining every
  aspect of the service in a safe environment. The
  leadership has to initiate this with humility and
  teachability.

- Start the habit of asking preaching friends at
  other churches to listen to recordings of your
  sermons and give feedback. Maybe start a

network of two or three people who do this for each other regularly.

- Form a small group of representative people in your church to meet for a specified time to do sermon evaluation. This group should include a diversity of ages, genders, and educational levels. Be wise to not invite troublemakers, but also, don't just invite people who will be "yes men." Have them fill out the evaluation form, and then meet with this group weekly for six weeks. Do this once or twice a year.

The church at Berea was considered particularly noble and noteworthy because they carefully considered all that they heard from Paul, examining the word preached (Acts 17:10–12). If they were noble for evaluating the apostles, how much more should we apply the same approach to our own preaching? We should engage in a regular and thoughtful system of preaching evaluation to make a small step toward more faithful and effective sermons.

24

At Weddings and Funerals, Be a Guide

Whenever I've taken a tour—whether it was atop a roofless bus in London or with a walking guide at Hobbiton in New Zealand—I've noticed that not all tour guides are created equal. The bad kind of tour guide is one who is trying too hard: talking too much, using tired and formulaic tropes, trying to be the center of attention instead of highlighting the place you are touring. But a good tour guide is a delight—someone who understands and performs well her role as a guide. This is one who is experiencing the sights with those he is leading, a knowledgeable person who shares in the fascination and joy of the place.

I want you to think of being this kind of good guide when you approach the weighty task of preaching at and presiding over weddings and funerals. Both weddings and funerals are out-of-the-ordinary moments in our lives when people are drawn together because someone they care about is transitioning from one life stage to another. At these momentous occasions, the good pastor is a good guide. He is the one who leads people from one place to another, helping them see and understand and appreciate what they are experiencing. If there is any time the preaching should be small—in the sense of short—it is definitely then! The good pastor realizes that his role in this event is not primarily to teach but to guide.

What does this look like?

At weddings, being a good guide means the pastor gladly orchestrates a celebration, a joyful ceremony about love as a gift from God. The wedding pastor-guide remembers that this is not a time for heavy instruction, flexing biblical passages about what husbands and wives are supposed to do or about how difficult marriage can be. Those are appropriate subjects for the pre- and post-marital counseling room and sometimes for the regular pulpit. But no one at a wedding cares about hearing those words. Everyone is there, rightly, to celebrate love and the joining of two humans to become one flesh (therein lies a mystery; let it be so).

The good pastor-guide is not seeking to use the wedding to preach a forty-five-minute sermon to a bunch of unchurched people. No, he is inviting the couple and the witnesses into the beauty and goodness of love, God's very nature. This invitation into love is not syrupy and sentimental but is a serious joy. The guide paints a picture—using this couple's particular story—of the serious joy of love. Let that be the message.

At funerals, being a good guide means the pastor directs a commemoration, a weighty ceremony about life as a gift from God. The funeral pastor-guide is there to lead the gathered to remember and celebrate the goodness of a person's life—even if it may be buried under a lot of imperfections and failures. There is good in every human made in the image of God, and this should be celebrated. The pastor is there to help people articulate the confusion of their feelings, to give words to people's experiences so that they might learn how to go on in a world that is different because of this death. A funeral should be not syrupy and sentimental but a time of joyful seriousness. "It is better to go to the house of mourning than the house of feasting, for it is the end of all people and the living take it to heart" (Ecclesiastes 7:2). Those who remain are invited to see the goodness of life under God and to take it to heart. The God of life is offering all people life in himself through Jesus Christ. Let that be the message.

In other words, take weddings and funerals seriously and joyfully. Don't put on yourself the burden of saying everything you think the people present need to hear. Your role is to guide people lovingly by coming alongside them in this new place where they have found themselves. Guide them with your words so that they might see its beauty—a beauty that is made by the God who gives love and life.

♦ 25 ♦

Stealing as Sub-Creating

In 2011, the young writer Austin Kleon was asked to give a talk at a community college in upstate New York. It wasn't a big gig, and he wasn't a famous guy. He didn't write an elaborate research paper or technical piece designed to impress others. Instead, Kleon made a thoughtful list of "ten things I wish I'd heard when I was starting out." His creative talk began to go viral and became a delightful book that explores the struggles and joys of creating beautiful things.[16]

At the top of Kleon's original list was the provocative advice, "Steal like an artist."

Kleon notes that all kinds of artists—writers, musicians, painters—eventually realize that their creativity is really a necessary and good kind of stealing. Picasso said it this way: "Good artists copy. Great artists steal. Art is theft." T. S. Eliot noted that immature poets imitate, while great poets steal. Or most simply, reflecting on his own music David Bowie said, "I'm a tasteful thief."

Sermon writing as thievery? That doesn't sound like a very positive metaphor. But the point is profound. Sermons are an act of creativity. No matter your preferred preaching style, denominational tradition, or individual personality, sermonizing is a creative act. And all creativity involves a necessary kind of stealing.

How so? Both aspects of sermonizing (writing and delivery) are possible for humans because we alone are made in the image of the God who creates. Divine-image-bearing humans participate in God's creativity by creating beautiful things, including sermons.

But there is a crucial difference between our creativity and God's. God's alone is *ex nihilo*—out of nothing. God's creating is not stealing. Ours necessarily is. Our creating is always a mash up, a bringing together of other ideas, metaphors, texts, materials, and images to communicate something good and life giving to others. We are, to use Tolkien's famous phrase, "sub-creators." Thus, our writing and preaching of sermons is a miraculous, creative act. And it's theft.

This creative mashing up of others' ideas and insights is what Austin Kleon means by saying that to be creative we should unashamedly "steal like an artist." We should not be surprised or ashamed that our sermonizing is dependent on others. Our work is never more than the labor of an apprentice in the workshop of a master artist.

So what impact does recognizing this artistic thievery have on our preaching? Let's sum it up with one simple sentence:

Happily and wisely learn from others.

You can't write sermons alone. You don't have to come up with all new ideas in your sermons. (In fact, that's probably a very bad idea.) You should gladly look to other people's insights to help you minister well in the pulpit. In fact, leaning on others' insights is not only wise, it is also honoring to the gifts that God has given our fellow humans.

This happy learning from others means:

- Reading and listening to good sermons, studying commentaries, and having intentional conversations with other readers, thinkers, and pastors.

- Reading widely, both non-fiction and, especially, great fiction. I often joke that I work as a professor and pastor just so I can support my novel-reading habit. But joking aside, I think my preaching, teaching, and thinking are immeasurably stronger because so much of my time is given to great stories.

- Focusing on the craft of writing. One tip for learning to write well is to physically copy out great lines from others' books, paying attention to how great sentences are crafted. You should also read good writing aloud, feeling its rhythm and pace and timbre.

• Analyzing what works rhetorically in others' sermons and trying it.

It means making small preaching steps!

Of course, you can do this foolishly and nefariously, and that's called plagiarism. You can easily fall off the dark edge of the "steal like an artist" mantra by becoming a mere secondhander, an ordinary thief. I've heard sermons and parts of sermons that I know were pilfered right from some more famous preacher without attribution. That's bad.

The simile is the key—steal *like* an artist, not like a petty burglar. To steal like an artist, to sermonize like an artist, means you acknowledge and rejoice in the help you receive from others, never acting like you are doing this on your own.

Once you recognize your sub-creating role, performed in community, you can live your preaching life with freedom, wrapping about your shoulders the comfortable and beautiful mantle of humility. What your people need from you is not the ability to come up with everything on your own. They need you to give your hours and your energy to learning—learning to steal like an artist.

Conclusion

We began this book by talking about the surprising goodness of smallness. When applied with intentionality in our lives, small is a great thing. In self-discipline, in sports, in relationships, or in preaching, small thoughtful steps are the way to make real and lasting change. I hope this small book has inspired you to make some of these steps.

In recent months I have gotten serious about golf. Any of you who know golf know that this is a sport that easily invites reflections on "life lessons." The way the game is structured and played, golf is ripe with metaphors and principles that apply beyond the sport itself. So too with the principle of small. Golf is very much a game of small, and when you attend to small things, great progress can be made. Though you would think that swinging a stick at a ball and making it go straight would be pretty easy, golf is so tricky because of the myriad of small parts of your body that are involved. Your wrists, hips, eyes, shoulders, knees, spine, and feet all need to do the right thing at the right time, every time. Golf is definitely a small ball sport in every way. And when something isn't working, it is small adjustments that make a huge difference. By slightly adjusting my grip, the placement of my head and knees, the position of the club face, the tee height of the ball, tiny changes make a massive difference. So too with our life as preachers. Small adjustments are where we must focus our energy.

I've been reading a well-known golf psychology book by Bob Rotella entitled *Golf Is Not a Game of Perfect.*[17] Rotella notes that if our expectation when playing golf is that every shot, every landing, and every putt will be perfect, then in our frustration at failing to meet that expectation we will lose the joy of the game. Instead, golfers must learn to love the challenge of every shot, embracing the fact that the alternatives—anger, fear, whining, and cheating—are no good and do no good to improve your game. The application of this wisdom to our lives in general is clear. Indeed, Rotella himself later wrote a similar book with the adjusted title *Life is Not a Game of Perfect.*[18]

Happily stealing like a good artist (see chapter 25), I want to apply this to our preaching. Preaching is not a game of perfect. No sermon will be perfect, and no lifetime of preaching will be without failures, missteps, missed opportunities, and imperfections. But that's okay. Our call is to faithfulness, not perfection, to joyful service, not hand-wringing anxiety. This vision for preaching should be lived and refined over the course of our ministries and small steps are the way forward, starting today.

So maybe you get criticized after a sermon and you lose your cool. Or you get praised and it begins to go to your head. Or maybe you try starting a "band of brothers" sermon-planning group and it fizzles out. Or you try manuscripting your sermon and it feels very clunky. <u>All of this is okay</u>. Preaching is not a game of perfect. Keep making small steps toward true, good, and beautiful preaching. This is what being faithful as a preacher looks like.

Regardless of where you find yourself in the world and in ministry right now, today is the moment to be intentional about the task of preaching. Regardless of whether you are an old expert or a first-year preacher, and regardless of whether you are preaching to twenty-five people online or 1000 in person, this is the time to make small steps toward better preaching. Join with me on the journey.

Acknowledgments

Though this book is small, a significant number of people have helped me along the way, and I want to acknowledge their gifts. My own homiletics professors from Trinity Evangelical Divinity School, Mike Bullmore and Greg Scharf, were always extremely kind and encouraging to me. I've never forgotten Dr. Bullmore pulling me aside after my first lab sermon and speaking life-giving words to me about my calling and giftedness. His kind words have stuck with me. Dr. Scharf has continued to encourage me from afar over the years, including graciously reading through most of the essays in this book and giving constructive feedback.

It is a gift and joy to share the pulpit with Pastor Kevin Jamison at Sojourn East. He is the lead pastor and he did not have to invite me to join him in the preaching ministry, but in humility and joy, he has. The result has been a beautiful partnership where each of us brings our own style to the pulpit while also constantly collaborating on the vision and content of sermons. We are also very fortunate to be part of a citywide collective of Sojourn churches where we share resources, ideas, and sermon manuscripts in an enriching band-of-brothers way.

Almost any book you read from me over the last five years has on it the invisible fingerprints of my former administrative assistant and still friend, Anna Poole Mondal. She has been a constant source of vivacious encouragement and has kindly lent her keen editorial eye to every essay in this book.

Finally, this book is dedicated to my wife of twenty-seven-plus years, Tracy Pennington. As the dedicatory note indicates, my sermons can be evaluated into two categories—those I talked with her about beforehand and those that I did not. There is a clear and consistent difference in the quality of these two types! She is a unique person who sees through all of my bluster, laziness, self-reliance, and surface-talk, always pushing me to go for the heart, to ask what God is saying (not what Professor Pennington wants to say), and to minister grace and kindness to those weary and hurting. She is a gift to me and, unbeknownst to them, a gift to all those I minister to.

Endnotes

Introduction

1 James Lang, *Small Teaching: Everyday Lessons from the Science of Learning* (Hoboken, NJ: Jossey-Bass, 2016).

Chapter 1: Handle Praise Carefully and Gladly

2 Emily Dickinson, "Fame is a Bee," in *The Poems of Emily Dickinson*, ed. R. W. Franklin (Cambridge: Harvard University Press, 1999).

Chapter 4: Pastoring as Conducting

3 Shankar Vedantam, "Do Orchestras Really Need Conductors?," *All Things Considered, November 27, 2012*, https://www.npr.org/sections/deceptivecadence/2012/11/27/165677915/do-orchestras-really-need-conductors.

4 Tom Service, quoted in Clemency Burton-Hill, "What Does a Conductor Actually Do?," http://www.bbc.com/culture/story/20141029-what-do-conductors-actually-do.

5 Burton-Hill, "What Does a Conductor Actually Do?"

6   Benjamin Zander, "The Transformative Power of Classical Music," TED Talk, https://www.npr.org/2017/11/10/562884481/benjamin-zander-how-does-music-transform-us.

Chapter 5: Be God's Witness, Not His Lawyer

7   E. Stanley Jones, quoted in Ruth A. Tucker, *From Jerusalem to Irian Jaya: A Biographical History of Christian Missions* (Grand Rapids: Zondervan, 2011), 331.

Chapter 7: Encaustic Preaching

8   The original inspiration for this metaphor came from a stimulating conversation with my brilliant friend and colleague Dr. Matthew Westerholm.

Chapter 8: Manuscript Writing as Thinking

9   Annie Dillard, *The Writing Life* (New York: Harper & Row, 1989), 2–3.

10 This metaphor came from my own experience. Only sometime after writing this essay was I alerted to a homiletics book with the title *Scripture Sculpture* by Ramesh Richard (Grand Rapids: Baker Books, 1995).

Chapter 11: The Rhythm of Education and the Jigsaw Puzzle

11 This essay is happily dependent on chapter 5 in Ronald J. Allen's excellent book, *The Teaching Sermon* (Nashville: Abingdon, 1995).

12   Anne Lamott, "12 Truths I Learned from Life and Writing," TED2017, https://www.ted.com/talks/anne_lamott_12_truths_i_learned_from_life_and_writing/transcript#t-408188.

Chapter 15: The First Minute of a Sermon

13   Check out my *Cars, Coffee, Theology YouTube channel.*

14   Lang, *Small Teaching*, 48.

Chapter 20: Every Sermon a Story

15   Another version of this graph and a fuller discussion of how stories work can be found in Jonathan T. Pennington, *Reading the Gospels Wisely: A Narrative and Theological Introduction* (Grand Rapids: Baker Academic, 2012).

Chapter 25: Stealing as Sub-Creating

16   Austin Kleon, *Steal Like an Artist: 10 Things Nobody Told You about Being Creative* (New York: Workman, 2012).

17   Bob Rotella with Bob Cullen, *Golf Is Not a Game of Perfect* (New York: Simon & Schuster, 1995).

18   Bob Rotella with Bob Cullen, *Life Is Not a Game of Perfect* (New York: Simon & Schuster, 1999).